First published in the US in 2026 by
Welbeck Children's Books
An imprint of Hachette Children's Group

Copyright © 2025 Hodder & Stoughton Limited

Author: Emily Stead
Designer: Jonathan Finch

All rights reserved. This book is sold subject to the condition that it may not be reproduced, stored in a retrieval system, or transmitted in any form or by any means, electronic, mechanical, photocopying, recording, or otherwise, without the publisher's prior consent.

A CIP catalogue record for this book is available from the British Library.

ISBN 978 1 80453 924 8

Printed in China
10 9 8 7 6 5 4 3 2 1

Welbeck Children's Books
An imprint of Hachette Children's Group
Part of Hodder & Stoughton Limited
Carmelite House, 50 Victoria Embankment
London EC4Y 0DZ

An Hachette UK Company
www.hachette.co.uk
www.hachettechildrens.co.uk

DISCLAIMER
All trademarks, brands, company names, team names, registered names, individual names, products, logos, and catchphrases used or cited in this book are the property of their respective owners and used in this book for informational and identifying purposes only. This book is a publication of Welbeck Children's Limited and has not been licensed, approved, sponsored, or endorsed by any person or entity.

The publishers would like to thank the following sources for their kind permission to reproduce the pictures in this book.

Getty Images: Aitor Alcalde/FIFA 74BR; Gabriel Aponte 51TR; Raul Arboleda/AFP 51BL; Ayman Aref/NurPhoto 33BL; Chris Arjoon/AFP 68BL; Gonzalo Arroyo/FIFA 75BR; Naomi Baker 34TR; Naomi Baker/The FA 26L; Robbie Jay Barratt/AMA 59BR; Al Bello 43TL; Daniel Beloumou Olomo/AFP 54TR; Shaun Botterill 27TR; Karl Bridgeman/The FA 6-7; Chris Brunskill/Fantasista 30TR; Simon Bruty/Anychance 36R; Alex Burstow/Arsenal FC 10TR; Giuseppe Cacace/AFP 55TR; Rodrigo Caillaud/Eurasia Sport Images 50B; Lynne Cameron/The FA 49TL; Alex Caparros/FIFA 74L; Ramsey Cardy/Sportsfile/UEFA 71BL; Jean Catuffe 28TR, 66B; Chung Sung-Jun 55BL; Piero Cruciatti/AFP 64TR; Carl de Souza/AFP 44R; Oscar Del Pozo/AFP 60L; Daniel Derajinski/Icon Sport 67TR; Tony Duffy/Allsport 35TR; Elsa 26R; Elsa/NWSL 69TR; Franck Fife/AFP 41, 42TR, 44BL, 46BR, 47TL, 66L, 77; Julian Finney/UEFA 4, 70BL; Toni Galan 73TR; Ewen Gavet/Icon Sport 67BL; James Gill/Danehouse 19BL; Alex Gottschalk/DeFodi Images 39T; Rich Graessle/Icon Sportswire 29TR; Pascal Guyot/AFP 21TR; Matthias Hangst 62L; Morgan Harlow/The FA 59BL; Image Photo Agency 64C, 65BR; Catherine Ivill/AMA 29BL; Catherine Ivill/UEFA 71TR; Daniel Jayo 42BR; Kirill Kudryavtsev/AFP 43BL, 76; Harriet Lander/Chelsea FC 28L; Harriet Lander/FIFA 46L; Philippe Le Tellier/Paris Match 35L; Andy Lyons 27BL; Stuart MacFarlane/Arsenal FC 57; Marcio Machado/Eurasia Sport Images 10BR; David Madison 53BR; Jure Makovec/AFP 32TR; Matt McNulty/UEFA 38R; Melinda Meijer/ISI Photos 68TR; Indranil Mukherjee/AFP 55L; Guang Niu 34BR; Christina Pahnke/sampics 62BR; Alex Pantling/UEFA 48; John Peters/Manchester United 58BL; Matthew Peters/Manchester United 35BR; Popperfoto 9TL, 9TR, 9C; Daniela Porcelli 45T, 63B; Daniela Porcelli/ISI Photos 47B; Stefan Postles 65TR; David Price/Arsenal FC 13BR, 58TR, 72; Manuel Queimadelos/Quality Sport Images 61L, 70TR; Ben Radford /Allsport 54BC; David Ramos 19TR, 34BL, 61R; David Ramos/FIFA 73BL; Ben Roberts Photo 39L; Sandra Ruhaut/Icon Sport 75T; Fadel Senna/AFP 60BR; Justin Setterfield 23B; Ezra Shaw 20, 80; Brad Smith/ISI Photos 53TR; Andreas Solaro/AFP 64BR; Andrea Staccioli/Insidefoto/LightRocket 15TR; Catherine Steenkeste 16-17; Rich Storry/NWSL 69BR; Selim Sudheimer 63TR; Bob Thomas Sports Photography 9BR, 22TR; Mark Thompson 31BR; John Todd/ISI Photos 38B; Pius Utomi Ekpei/AFP 54BR; Joan Valls/Urbanandsport/NurPhoto 31L; Omar Vega 52; Claudio Villa 24-25, 27L; Visionhaus 58BR; Darren Walsh/Chelsea FC 22BL, 36L; William West/AFP 33TR; Sebastian Widmann/UEFA 21BR; James Worsfold 18L; Mustafa Yalcin/Anadolu Agency 33BR

Shutterstock: BRG.photography 23L; Dedraw Studio 1, 3, 26B, 28B, 30B, 32B; Eugene B-sov 50TR; Golden Sikorka 11BL; grey_and 27TL; Jackreznor 11TR; Nattawit Khomsanit 15TL; Kotoimages 14; Igor Kyrlytsya 31TR; Alberto Martin/EPA 21BL; Master1305 13T; Member 11L; MockupMonster 15BL; moondes 10TL; natrot 37L, 37R, 37BL, 37BR; A.Paes 13BL; Refox Photos 15BR, 18R; SL-Photography 8; vectorlight 45B; Yuri A/PeopleImages 23TR

Every effort has been made to acknowledge correctly and contact the source and/or copyright holder of each picture and Welbeck Publishing Group apologises for any unintentional errors or omissions, which will be corrected in future editions of this book.

The Junior FOOTBALL Encyclopedia

WELBECK
CHILDREN'S BOOKS

Contents

- The beautiful game — 6
- How football began — 8
- Football rules — 10
- Football kit — 14

1 Football skills

- Ball control, passing — 18
- Shooting, dribbling, tackling, heading — 20
- Set pieces — 22

2 Pitch positions

- Goalkeepers — 26
- Defenders — 28
- Midfielders — 30
- Forwards — 32

| Record breakers | 34 |

| Tactics and formations | 36 |

| Super stadiums | 38 |

3 Top tournaments

The World Cup	42
The Women's World Cup	44
The Olympic Games	46
Europe	48
South America	50
North and Central America	52
Africa	54
Asia	55

4 Football around the world

England	58
Spain	60
Germany	62
Italy	64
France	66
United States	68

| The Champions League | 70 |

| Cup competitions | 72 |

| More football! | 74 |

| Glossary | 76 |

The beautiful game

Football is the world's most popular sport! Huge crowds travel to see football matches played in stadiums, with many more fans watching on TV. Two teams, each with 11 players, must kick a ball into a goal to score. The team that scores the most goals wins the match.

How football began

People have played ball games for thousands of years, all over the world. Many of these games helped to shape how football is played today. Here's how…

3,000 years ago
The ancient Maya people played a game called 'pitz'. Players scored by passing a rubber ball through a carved stone hoop using their arms or hips.

900 years ago
In medieval England, whole villages of peasants joined in to kick an inflated pig's bladder. Matches were so noisy that King Edward II banned London games in 1314!

2,800 years ago
'Episkyros' was played by the Ancient Greeks. It is an early form of football, but players could use their arms to move the ball.

2,000 years ago
'Cuju' was a game played long ago in China. The name means 'kick-ball'. Players had to kick a leather ball stuffed with feathers.

200 years ago
Pupils in English public schools in the 19th century played a game that was a cross between modern football and rugby. Every school had its own set of rules.

over 150 years ago
In October 1863, the rules of modern football were written down for the first time by the English Football Association. One important rule was that players could not carry the ball with their hands!

Football first

The first international match was played between Scotland and England in Glasgow, Scotland, in 1872. Up to four thousand fans came to watch at Hamilton Crescent cricket ground. The score was 0–0.

A growing game

Towards the end of the 19th century, workers who travelled around the British Empire introduced football to countries in Africa, South America, Asia and beyond. More countries began to organise their own competitions.

In the early days of football, players wore woollen stockings, long trousers and thick cotton jerseys.

Did you know?

Asian nations Japan and Siam (now Thailand) entered the first World Cup in 1930, held in Uruguay, but decided not to play. Egypt missed the tournament as their ship was late because of a storm!

Women's football

Can you believe it? In the 20th century, women were banned from playing professional football in many countries for around 50 years! Now women's football is growing again, with more professional leagues and competitions than ever before. More than 30 million women and girls now play football around the world.

The United States won the first Women's World Cup in 1991, more than 60 years after the men's tournament was first held.

Football rules

Many of the rules of football were first written down in 1863, by the English FA. More rules have been added over the years.

Substitutes

Up to five more players can join the game as substitutes. They replace teammates who are injured or tired, or are brought on to help the team's tactics. Substitutes sit in seats known as the bench.

Teams

Each team is made up of 11 players. One is a goalkeeper and the other ten are called **outfield** players. Matches cannot be played with fewer than seven players a side.

Coaching staff

The coach or manager is in charge of the team. They pick which players to play and decide the match tactics. Assistant coaches and a medical team are part of the coaching staff too.

Did you know?

Carlo Ancelotti is the only manager to win all five of Europe's top leagues, in Italy, England, France, Spain and Germany.

The field of play

A football pitch is rectangular and marked with white lines. Football pitches can be different sizes, but they need to be a certain size for professional matches. The playing surface is most often grass, but artificial turf is popular too.

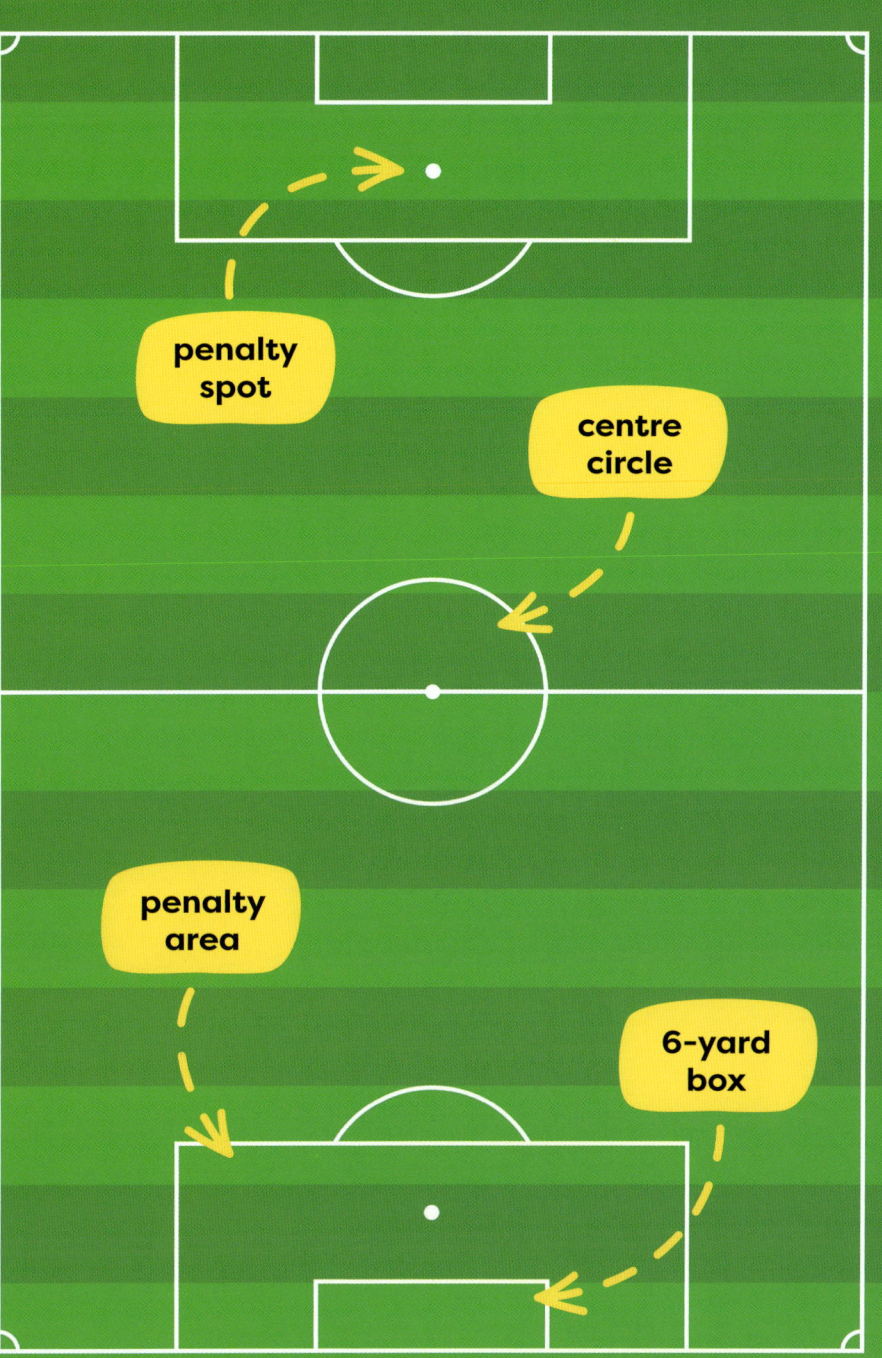

- penalty spot
- centre circle
- penalty area
- 6-yard box

The length of the pitch must measure between 90 and 120 metres (100–130 yards), and its width between 45 and 90 metres (50–100 yards).

Tall floodlights in stadiums mean that matches can be played safely at night.

Under-soil heating

Many pitches around the world have under-soil heating below the playing surface. Hot water travels through pipes, which stops the pitch from freezing during cold weather.

Football rules

The referee
The referee makes sure that the game is played according to the rules. They have a whistle to attract the players' attention, and a stopwatch to time the game correctly. They write important facts about the game in a notebook.

Cards
The referee can show a yellow or red card to any player who commits a serious foul.

yellow card — The yellow card is a warning. The player can play on, but two yellow cards means an automatic red card.

red card — The player must leave the pitch straight away, and cannot return.

A straight red card can be shown without a yellow card first.

Assistant referees

Two assistant referees run up and down the **touchlines** and carry a flag. They help the main referee and can talk to them through a headset. They help decide throw-ins and when players are offside. A fourth official is in charge of substitutions.

Goal or no goal?

Cameras in the goal record when the ball has crossed the goal-line. A signal is sent to the referee's watch to tell them whether or not a goal should be awarded. This is called goal-line technology (GLT).

VAR

Some competitions have an extra Video Assistant Referee (VAR). This referee watches video clips of the match to check that the referee on the pitch has made the right decision.

Football kit

Footballers don't need a lot of expensive equipment to play the sport they love. Here is some of the basic kit.

shirt and shorts
Football kits are made from lightweight fabrics that are comfortable to move about in and that keep players cool and dry.

socks
Long socks that can hold shin pads in place.

football
In professional football, footballs must be a certain size and weight. Younger players play with smaller-sized balls, depending on how old they are.

boots

Footballers wear special boots with studs on the sole to help grip the pitch. Studs are usually made from plastic or metal. Players choose which type of boot to wear according to the surface of the pitch.

base layers

In cold weather, tops and leggings called base layers or skins can be worn underneath football kits. They help keep to muscles warm and avoid injuries, and move sweat away from the body.

Did you know?

Some kits are made from recycled polyester, using recycled plastic bottles.

water bottle

Water is the best drink to replace the fluids lost while playing football. Not drinking enough water can make players **dehydrated**. Fizzy or sugary drinks are not good choices when playing sport.

shin pads

These are designed to protect the shin bone from contact with the ball and from other players. All players must wear shin pads to prevent injuries.

1 Football skills

Footballers need to learn a range of skills if they want to become professional players. It takes years of working on skills like passing, shooting, tackling, dribbling and heading in training to reach the very top. The best football players are brilliant at controlling the ball.

FOOTBALL SKILLS

Ball control

Ball control, passing and shooting are three key skills that players must learn from a young age. Working hard on these skills in training helps players to be at their best when playing matches.

Being able to control the ball well is important whatever your position on the pitch. The best players are comfortable controlling the ball with both feet and can use different parts of the foot.

Parts of the foot

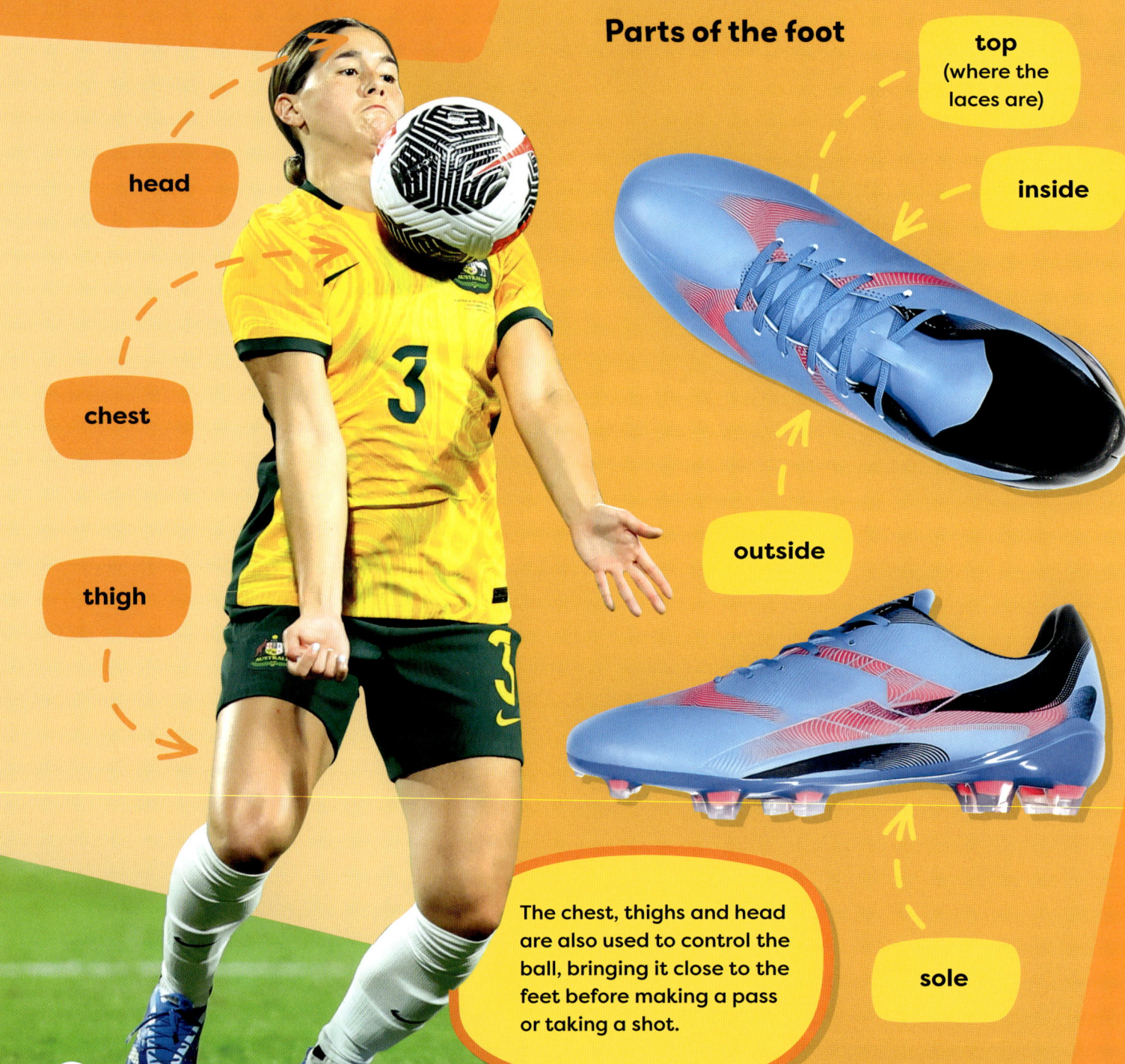

- head
- chest
- thigh
- top (where the laces are)
- inside
- outside
- sole

The chest, thighs and head are also used to control the ball, bringing it close to the feet before making a pass or taking a shot.

Passing

Passing the ball between teammates is the best way to keep possession. Players move the ball up the pitch until they create a chance to score. Passes can be made on the ground or in the air.

Did you know?

Some teams make more than 1,000 passes during a match!

Shooting

Shooting is when a player strikes the ball at goal. Players can take shots from anywhere on the pitch, but shots inside the penalty area are more likely to be on target. Shots also include headers on goal.

Accuracy

Striking through the centre of the ball with the inside of the shooting foot makes shots more accurate.

Power

To create power in their shots, players often hit the ball with the top of the foot (where the laces are). After kicking the ball, their shooting leg follows through in the direction of the goal.

Did you know?

The fastest shots in football can reach speeds of up to 210 km per hour (131 miles per hour).

FOOTBALL SKILLS

Dribbling, tackling and heading the ball are three more important skills that players use in training and in matches.

Dribbling

Dribbling is the skill of moving the ball while running, taking small touches to move it forwards up the pitch. Players need to have good ball control and be skilled at using both feet.

Head up
Players should keep their head up while dribbling, so they don't run into danger.

Shoulder switch
Players can drop a shoulder and pretend to move in one direction, before racing off with the ball the opposite way.

Fast feet
Strong dribblers take lots of touches using the inside and outside of their feet to control the ball.

Throw-ins

When the ball goes out of play over either touchline, a throw-in is taken to restart play. Keeping both feet on the ground, players must throw the ball from behind their head using both hands.

Penalty kicks

A penalty kick is awarded when a foul by the defending team takes place within the penalty area. These are one-on-one shots against the goalkeeper.

Penalty shoot-out

A penalty shoot-out is often used when the score is a draw in a tournament, to decide who wins. A shoot-out often takes place after a period of extra time.

Each team takes five penalty kicks. If the scores are still level after this, teams take more penalty kicks in turn until one team wins.

2 Pitch positions

Football teams are made up of 11 players, who take their places in different positions on the pitch. Each player has their own job to do to help the team. Teams have one goalkeeper, while the other ten players are a mix of defenders, midfielders and forwards.

PITCH POSITIONS

Goalkeepers

A goalkeeper is only the only player on the team who is allowed to use their hands to touch the ball, but only in their own penalty area. They need to be good with their hands as well as their feet to stop the ball from hitting the back of their net. They are sometimes called the 'last line of defence.'

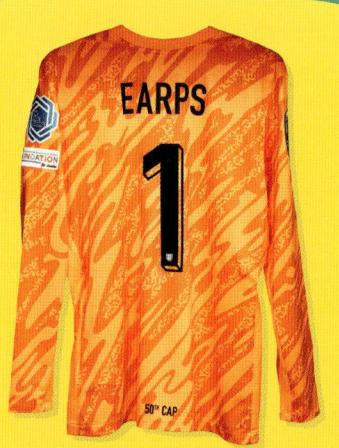

Keeper's kit

Goalkeepers wear a different coloured jersey from their teammates so the referee can see who has handled the ball in a crowd of players. The number on the back of is often 1 or 13.

Emi Martínez was voted the best goalkeeper in the world 2024 and the second best in 2023.

Top skills

- Shot-stopping
- Catching crosses
- Diving
- Kicking out
- Throwing
- Quick reflexes

Special gloves help goalkeepers grip the ball and protect their hands and wrists from injuries.

Alisson Becker's quick thinking and perfect passes create chances for his teammates to score.

Staying alert

Goalkeepers sometimes don't touch the ball for long periods of time during a match. They must stay focused and be ready to make a save. Keepers can start a quick attack for their own side too, by launching a long throw or kick to catch opponents off guard.

Cleaning up

USA goalkeeper Alyssa Naeher kept **clean sheets** in the finals of both the 2019 World Cup and the Paris 2024 Olympics to help her country become champions.

Did you know?

Goalkeepers don't need to run around as much as other players during a match. The energy they save over the years means they often have a longer football career than their teammates.

PITCH POSITIONS

Defenders

Defenders have the job of stopping their opponents from scoring a goal. Teams can play with three, four or five defenders depending on their **tactics**. There are different types of defenders: central defenders, full-backs, sweepers, and wing-backs who line up together in front of the goalkeeper.

Netherlands captain Virgil van Dijk is one of the world's most skilful defenders. He plays in central defence.

Worth a million

In January 2025, USA central defender Naomi Girma made history by becoming the first female footballer to cost over $1 million dollars (about £900,000). Her move from San Diego Wave to Chelsea set a new world record in the women's game.

Top skills

- Tackling
- Heading
- Positioning
- Passing
- Clearing the ball
- Strength

Quick as a flash

Sometimes a team's quickest players play in defence. Left-back Alphonso Davies is known for his incredible speed when defending and attacking down the **wing**.

Lionesses legend

Lucy Bronze is a right wing-back who loves to help the attack. She has played more than 130 matches for England's Lionesses and scored more than 15 goals, too.

Did you know?

Defenders, and centre-backs in particular, make excellent team captains. They have a good view of the whole pitch and can shout instructions to their teammates.

PITCH POSITIONS

Midfielders

Midfielders play between their team's defenders and forwards, in the middle of the pitch. There are different types of midfielder, but all must have strong passing skills and plenty of energy. The number of midfielders in a team depends on its formation.

Spain and Manchester City midfielder Rodri is a master at winning the ball in midfield for club and country.

Defensive duties

The job of a defensive midfielder is to break up the opposition's attack. They must read the game well to predict how teams will try to move forwards with the ball. They try to stop passes and make important tackles. They play just in front of their team's defence.

Wide midfielder

Wide midfielders play close to the touchline on either the left or the right of the pitch. They make chances for other players to score by putting crosses into the box, or they take shots themselves.

Top skills

- Passing
- Tackling
- Ball control
- Dribbling
- Creativity
- Positioning

Midfield engine

A central midfielder operates in the middle of the pitch. They are sometimes called the 'engine' of the team as they work hard to link the defence and the attack. They make lots of passes during a match and often do the most running over a game.

This heatmap shows where this midfielder spent their time during a match. The red areas are where they spent the most time.

On the attack

Attacking midfielders are often the team's most creative players. They need to be good at all different types of passes to create chances for their teammates to score. Central attacking midfielders are sometimes called 'playmakers'.

Playmaker Aitana Bonmatí has won the Ballon d'Or trophy twice.

Did you know?

Midfielder David Beckham's crossing skills were so good, they inspired the name of a film: *Bend It Like Beckham*!

PITCH POSITIONS

Forwards

The forwards on a team have the task of creating and scoring goals. There are different types of forwards. The centre forward or striker plays furthest forward, wingers attack down the left and right and sides of the pitch, and the second striker (No.10) plays in the space behind the main striker.

Super striker

Striker Erling Haaland may not make many touches during a match, but his goal-scoring record is among the best players in history.

Did you know?

In modern football, forwards must also help defend. They try to stop the opposition's goalkeeper and defenders from moving the ball up the pitch.

Top skills

- Shooting
- Heading
- Crossing
- Dribbling
- Speed
- Agility

Goal queen

Khadija 'Bunny' Shaw is Jamaica's all-time top goalscorer for both the women and men's teams. She holds the ball up well and has a deadly strike.

Kylian Mbappé won the Golden Boot at the 2022 World Cup in Qatar. His eight goals helped France reach the final.

Wing wonder

Egypt's Mohamed Salah scores a fantastic amount of goals playing on the right wing. Not only is his shooting deadly, but he magics up many **assists** for his teammates.

Golden boot

Many tournaments and leagues award a special trophy called the Golden Boot (or Shoe) to the player that has scored the most goals during the competition.

Record breakers

Since the modern game began, fans around the world have watched their heroes achieve some incredible feats in football. Many records have stood for decades and may never be beaten.

Most international goals
(men or women)
190
Christine Sinclair
(Canada)

Most goals in a calendar year
91
Lionel Messi
(Barcelona), in 2012

Most international appearances
(men or women)
354
Kristine Lilly
(United States)

Youngest World Cup winner
17 years and **249** days old

Pelé (Brazil),
1958 tournament

Most clean sheets
(all seasons)
537
Ray Clemence
(Scunthorpe Utd, Liverpool and Tottenham Hotspur),
from 1965–88

Most major trophies
(coach)
49
Alex Ferguson

Most international trophies
22
Argentina

3 World Cup wins
16 Copa América wins
1 Confederations Cup champions win
2 CONMEBOL–UEFA Cup wins

Tactics and formations

Football coaches choose different tactics and formations to try to get the best result in a match.

Team tactics
Teams that have good technical players often focus on keeping hold of the ball and passing it around. This is called keeping **possession**.

Some teams play **counter-attacking** football. Instead of trying to keep possession, they use their speedy players to quickly launch an attack when their opponents lose the ball.

Other teams play a more **direct** style of football. Instead of making lots of passes from the defence to midfield to the forwards, long balls are launched from the goalkeeper or defence towards the forwards. The forwards use their strength and height to try to win the ball.

Coaches can change their tactics during a match if they need to.

Four formations

A formation is how a team is set up on the pitch, broken down into rows of defenders, midfielders and forwards. For 11-a-side football, the numbers add up to 10. The goalkeeper is not included.

What do the numbers mean?

4 - 3 - 3

The number of defenders. | The number of midfielders. | The number of forwards.

4-3-3
This formation is often used by many of the world's top teams. It is a more attacking formation with three forwards who can create more chances to score.

4-4-2
A classic formation that gives teams a good balance in defence and attack. It is not as popular as it once was, but many teams still line up this way.

4-2-3-1
This set-up is more defensive, with four defenders and two defensive midfielders. Three attacking midfielders and a striker complete the line-up.

3-5-2
Three central defenders form a strong defence. Two wing-backs are part of a midfield five, while two strikers try to score.

Super stadiums

Fans have gathered in stadiums to watch sport for thousands of years. Today, clubs and national teams have their own modern stadiums so that thousands of fans can come and watch matches. Some stadiums can seat more than 100,000 fans!

Did you know?

The modern Wembley Stadium was built on the same site as the original stadium that had stood from 1923 until 2003. It reopened in 2007 with 90,000 seats. It is home to England's men's and women's national teams.

USA's largest football stadium

The Rose Bowl in California is a huge stadium that can hold up to 92,000 spectators. It hosts all kinds of sports including baseball and American football, but it's most famous in the football world for hosting the 1994 World Cup final.

Shared stadium

The most famous stadium shared by two teams can be found in Milan, Italy. The San Siro stadium (also called the Stadio Giuseppe Meazza) has been the home ground of both AC Milan and Internazionale since 1947.

Oldest stadium

The world's oldest football stadium that is still used today is Sandygate in Sheffield, England. The first competitive game played at the ground took place on 26 December 1860. The two teams were Hallam and Sheffield FC.

Sky-high stadium

The Estadio Daniel Alcides Carrión in Cerro de Pasco, Peru, is the highest altitude stadium in the world. It was built 4,380 m (14,370 ft) above sea level. Playing football is difficult there, as there is less oxygen to breathe.

3 Top tournaments

Some of the biggest tournaments and prizes in sport belong to football. The ultimate tournament in both the men's and women's games is the World Cup, while each continent has its own competition to decide a champion. Football is an Olympic sport too, with the chance for players to win more medals for their country.

Triple header

Three nations were chosen to host the World Cup in 2026 together: the United States, Canada and Mexico. The MetLife Stadium in New Jersey, United States, was selected to stage the final.

Billions of fans

More than 5 billion people watched the 2022 World Cup on TV or online. That's more than half the world's population! Close to 1.5 billion fans watched the final between Argentina and France.

Portugal's Cristiano Ronaldo became the first man to score at five different World Cups at the 2022 tournament.

World Cup records

Most wins
5 - Brazil

Winning nations
Uruguay, Italy, Germany, Brazil, England, Argentina, France, Spain

Most appearances (tournaments)
5 - Lionel Messi (Argentina)
5 - Lothar Matthäus (Germany)
5 - Cristiano Ronaldo (Portugal)
5 - Rafael Marquez (Mexico)
5 - Andres Guardado (Mexico)

Most appearances (matches)
26 - Lionel Messi (Argentina)

Top scorer (all)
16 goals - Miroslav Klose (Germany)

Top scorer (single tournament)
13 goals - Just Fontaine (France)

TOP TOURNAMENTS

The Women's World Cup

Just like the men's competition, the Women's World Cup is the biggest tournament in women's football. It was first held in 1991 and was won by the United States. Nine tournaments have been played so far, with 32 nations now competing for World Cup glory.

Winning nations

The USA have a fantastic record at the Women's World Cup and have been crowned champions a record four times. Germany have two titles, and Japan and Norway have one each. Spain's women won their first trophy in 2023.

Spain beat England 1–0 in the final of the World Cup 2023 in Sydney, Australia.

Did you know?

The trophy awarded to the winners is not the original cup. The first trophy was stolen after Norway won it in 1995. The current cup, made from gold-plated brass, has been used since the 1999 tournament.

Brazil teammates Marta and Formiga are both former World Cup record-breakers.

World Cup records

Most wins
4 - United States

Winning nations
United States, Germany, Japan, Norway, Spain

Most appearances (tournaments)
7 - Formiga (Brazil)

Most appearances (matches)
30 - Kristine Lilly (United States)

Top scorer (all)
17 goals - Marta (Brazil)

Top scorer (single tournament)
10 goals - Michelle Akers (United States)

Global game

Australia and New Zealand hosted the 2023 Women's World Cup together. This was the first time the tournament was held in the Southern Hemisphere and by two countries. Brazil will host the 2027 competition, making it the first tournament to be played in South America.

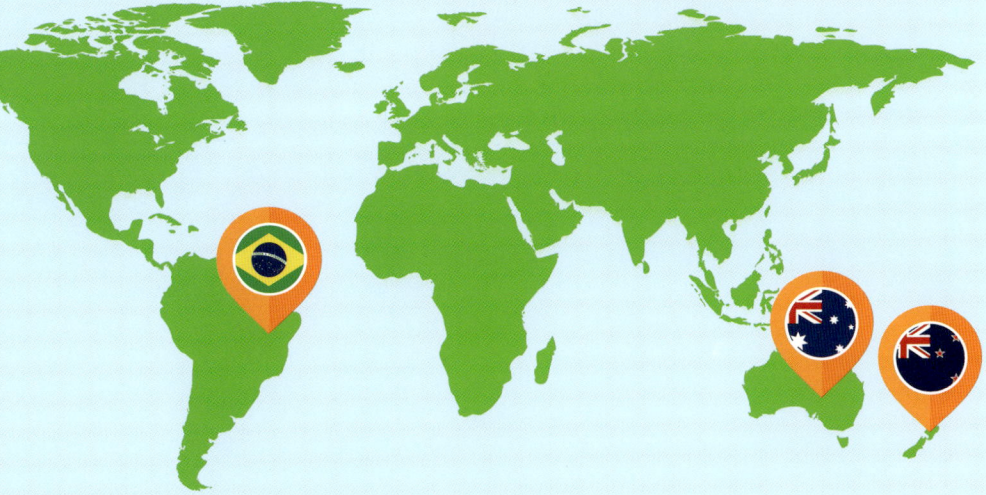

TOP TOURNAMENTS

The Olympic Games

Football became an Olympic sport at the Paris 1900 Games, decades before the first World Cup. A men's tournament has been played at every Games since, except one. The first time women were able to compete for an Olympic medal came much later, at the Atlanta 1996 games.

Tournament rules
Many famous male footballers don't play in the Olympic tournament. Instead, nations must choose young players under the age of 23 in their squads, with three over-23s allowed.

Going for gold
Shiny gold medals are awarded to the winners, the runners-up earn silver and the nation to finish in third place win bronze medals.

Spain's young stars won the country's first gold medal since 1992 at the Paris 2024 Games.

Gold rush

In the women's tournament, players of any age may play. Expect to see some of the world's best female footballers. In the eight tournaments played so far, the United States have won gold five times, including at the first ever competition in Atlanta 1996. They have won a silver and a bronze medal too.

Mallory Swanson struck the winning goal as USA beat Brazil in the final at Paris 2024 to win gold.

Did you know?

Brazil's women's side have lost three Olympic finals, defeated each time by the United States.

Olympic football records

Most gold medals

Men: Hungary, Great Britain – **both 3**

Women: United States – **5**

Most medals

Men: Brazil – **7**

Women: United States – **7**

Most matches played

Men: Brazil – **66**

Women: United States – **44**

Top scorer (all tournaments)

Men: Sophus Nielsen (Denmark) and Antal Dunai (Hungary) – **both 13 goals**

Woman: Cristiane (Brazil) – **14 goals**

Top scorer (single tournaments)

Men: Ferenc Bene (Hungary) – **12 goals**

Woman: Vivianne Miedema (Netherlands) – **10 goals**

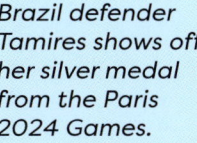

Brazil defender Tamires shows off her silver medal from the Paris 2024 Games.

TOP TOURNAMENTS

Europe

Both the European Championship and the Women's European Championship (called the Euros and Women's Euros for short) take place every four years. Nations compete to become champions of Europe, with 24 (men's) or 16 (women's) best international teams taking part in each tournament.

Top ten

Ten different teams have won the men's trophy since the competition began in 1960. Spain, Germany, Italy and France have all won multiple titles, while the Soviet Union, Czechoslovakia, Netherlands, Denmark, Greece and Portugal have each won once.

Spain are the current men's champions. They beat England 2–1 in the final of Euro 2024 in Germany.

Did you know?

England, the Republic of Ireland, Scotland and Wales will jointly host the next tournament, which will kick off in 2028.

Women's winners

Only five countries have ever won the Women's Euros. They are Germany, Norway, Sweden, Netherlands and England. Germany lead the way with eight trophies, winning the tournament six times in a row between 1995 and 2013. Norway are the next best nation with two trophies.

Lionesses roar to victory

When England hosted the Women's Euro 2022, their team nicknamed the Lionesses won every match they played. It was a dream come true to win their very first trophy at the famous Wembley Stadium in London.

Euros records

Most wins (tournaments)

Men: Spain – 4

Women: Germany – 8

Most matches played

Men: Germany – 58

Women: Germany – 46

Top scorer (all final tournaments)

Men: Cristiano Ronaldo (Portugal) – 14 goals

Women: Inka Grings and Birgit Prinz (both Germany) – 10 goals

Top scorer (single final tournaments)

Men: Michel Platini (France) – 9 goals

Woman: Inka Grings (Germany), Beth Mead (England) and Alexandra Popp (Germany) – 6 goals

Did you know?

Super coach Sarina Wiegman won the trophy with her home nation the Netherlands in 2017, and then again as England coach in 2022.

TOP TOURNAMENTS

South America

The men's Copa América is famous for being the oldest **continental** football competition that still runs today. The first tournament was held over a hundred years ago between four national teams from South America. Now 16 teams take part, with teams from other continents often invited to play.

Team treble
Only Argentina have won three Copa América tournaments in a row, between 1945 and 1947.

A plaque with the name of the winner is added to the base of the Copa América trophy after every final.

Copa América Femenina

The women's competition kicked off in 1991, with the hosts Brazil crowned the very first winners. Brazil have an almost perfect record in the competition, winning the trophy eight times altogether. In fact, they have only ever lost the tournament once, when Argentina beat them in the 2006 final.

Did you know?

In both men's and women's football, the Copa América champions play a one-off match against the European Champions for the chance to win the Finalissima trophy.

Young Colombia forward Linda Caicedo was voted the best player at the Copa América Femenina in 2022.

South America records

Most wins (tournaments)
Men: Argentina – 16
Women: Brazil – 8

Most matches played (tournaments)
Men: Uruguay – 212
Women: Argentina and Brazil – 50

Most tournaments played (player)
Men: Lionel Messi (Argentina) – 39
Women: Formiga (Brazil) – 6

Top scorer (all tournaments)
Men: Norberto Méndez (Argentina) and Zizinho (Brazil) – 17 goals
Women: Cristiane (Brazil) – 31 goals

Top scorer (single tournaments)
Men: Jair (Brazil), Humberto Maschio (Argentina) and Javier Ambrois (Uruguay) – 9 goals
Woman: Roseli (Brazil) – 16 goals

TOP TOURNAMENTS

North and Central America

For countries in North America, Central America and the Caribbean, the biggest tournament is called the Gold Cup. It is held every two years. Since the competition began in 1991, so far only three national teams have won it: the United States, Mexico and Canada.

Magical Mexico

In January 2025, USA Mexico held the record for the most tournament wins with nine titles. USA have seven titles and Canada have been champions once. All three nations are from North America.

Mexico beat Panama in the 2023 final to win the 2023 Gold Cup.

Men's Gold Cup records

Most wins (tournaments)

Mexico – 9

Most matches played (country)

Mexico – 125

Top scorer (all tournaments)

Landon Donovan (USA) – 18 goals

Top scorer (single tournament)

Luís Roberto Alves (Mexico) – 11 goals

CONCACAF W Championship records

Champions

United States – 9 times
Canada – 2 times

Runners-up

Canada – 6 times
Mexico – 2 times
Costa Rica, Brazil and New Zealand – all once

Most matches played (country)

United States – 44

Top scorer (single tournament)

Silvana Burtini (Canada) – 14 goals

The United States beat rivals Canada to claim the 2022 cup.

CONCACAF W Championship

The biggest competition for women's national teams in North and Central America is the **CONCACAF** W Championship. The W stands for 'Women's'. It has been known by a few different names since the first edition in 1991. After a qualifying stage, eight nations compete in a knockout tournament to try to win the trophy. The winners also earn their place at the Women's World Cup.

Did you know?

Only the United States and Canada have ever won the Championship. The United States have a record nine triumphs, while Canada have two titles.

TOP TOURNAMENTS

Africa

The Africa Cup of Nations (AFCON) and women's cup (WAFCON) are the top trophies for national teams in Africa. The men's competition dates back to 1957, while the first women's edition was held in 1991. Teams compete from all across Africa.

Ivory Coast, nicknamed the Elephants, beat Nigeria in the 2023 final to win their third AFCON title.

African record-breakers

Most wins (tournaments)

Men: Egypt – 7

Women: Nigeria – 11

Winning nations (more than one title)

Men: Egypt, Cameroon, Ghana, Nigeria, Ivory Coast, Algeria, DR Congo

Women: Nigeria, Equatorial Guinea

Top scorer (single tournaments)

Men: Ndaye Mulamba (DR Congo) – 9 goals

Women: Perpetua Nkwocha (Nigeria) – 11 goals

Top scorer (all)

Men: Samuel Eto'o (Cameroon) – 18 goals

Women: Perpetua Nkwocha (Nigeria) – 34 goals

Most matches

Rigobert Song holds the record for playing the most matches at AFCON. The Cameroon defender played in the tournament 36 times and later became the team's coach.

Nigeria's Perpetua Nkwocha (right) is the all-time top scorer at WAFCON.

Asia

The first men's Asian Cup took place in Hong Kong in 1956 with only 4 Asian teams. A tournament for women's international teams followed in 1975. Today, up to 24 teams take part in the men's tournament, with 12 in the women's edition. Both competitions take place every four years.

Qatar won their second Asian Cup in 2023 as the competition's host nation.

Champions China

No team comes close to matching China's record in the Women's Asian Cup. Their record of nine titles is easily the best in the competition's history.

Sam Kerr was just 16 when she helped Australia to win the Asian Cup in 2010. She scored in the final against North Korea.

Asian Cup records

Most wins (tournaments)

Men: Japan – 4

Women: China – 9

Winning teams
(more than one title)

Men: Japan, Saudi Arabia, Iran, South Korea, Qatar

Women: China, North Korea, Chinese Taipei, Japan

Top scorer (single tournaments)

Men: Almoez Ali (Qatar) – **9 goals**

Women: Yūki Nagasato (Japan), Jung Jung-suk (Republic of Korea), Li Ying (China), Sam Kerr (Australia), Ri Kum-suk (DPRK) – **7 goals**

Top scorer (all)

Ali Daei (Iran) – **14 goals**

4
Football around the world

Football is the number one sport across the globe, with professional football played on every continent except Antarctica. The most famous men's and women's leagues are currently found in Europe. Some of the world's best players now star in the top leagues in United States and Saudi Arabia too.

FOOTBALL IN ENGLAND

The Premier League

The top men's division in England is the Premier League. Its first season kicked off in 1992. Before that, the league was called the First Division. It's one of the fastest and most exciting leagues in the world. Many of the world's best players come to England to compete for the famous trophy.

Number of teams	20
Number of games each season	38
Clubs relegated each season	3

Premier League records

Most appearances
(all seasons)

Gareth Barry - 653 matches

Top scorer
(all seasons)

Alan Shearer - 260

Most titles

Manchester United hold the record for the most Premier League titles won. They have been crowned champions 13 times. The last time they won the trophy was in the 2012–13 season.

Did you know?

Manchester City coach Pep Guardiola is the only coach to lead his side to win four Premier League titles in a row. He and City set the incredible record between 2021 and 2024.

The Women's Super League

The highest division in England for women is the Women's Super League (WSL). 14 professional teams play in the league. Each season, the top three teams qualify for the Women's Champions League.

Women's Super League records

Most appearances (all seasons)

Jordan Nobbs - 200+ matches

Top scorer (all seasons)

Vivianne Miedema - 80+

Number of teams	12
Number of games each season	22
Clubs relegated each season	1

Top for trophies

Since the league became the WSL in 2011, Chelsea have won the most titles. The London club won six straight titles between 2020 and 2025, a WSL record!

Did you know?

Midfielder Jordan Nobbs has played more WSL matches than anyone else, playing for Arsenal and Aston Villa.

FOOTBALL IN SPAIN

La Liga

The top men's league in Spain is called La Liga. It was first formed almost 100 years ago. Ten teams played in the first season in 1929. Today, double the number of teams compete, with the bottom three teams relegated to the second division at the end of each season.

La Liga records

Most appearances (all seasons)
Andoni Zubizarreta and Joaquin both 622 matches

Most points in a season
Real Madrid (2011–12) and Barcelona (2012–13) - 100

Top scorer (all seasons)
Lionel Messi (Barcelona) - 474

Number of teams	20
Number of games each season	38
Clubs relegated each season	3

Kings of Spain

Real Madrid have won more La Liga titles than any other club. They have been champions more than 35 times. Barcelona are the next most successful club. Matches between these rival clubs are known as El Clásico (The Classic).

Real Madrid's riches allow them to buy the world's best players. Jude Bellingham's transfer fee was over one hundred million euros (about £88 million)!

Did you know?

Nine different teams have won La Liga's famous trophy.

Liga F

The Primera División de la Liga de Fútbol Femenino, known as Liga F for short, is the highest division for women's football in Spain. The league was founded in 1988 and it's now one of the most important women's leagues in Europe.

Did you know?

While twelve different clubs have been Liga F champions, Real Madrid have never won a title.

Midfielder Aitana Bonmatí has played for Barcelona since she joined their academy at the age of 13.

Number of teams	16
Number of games each season	30
Clubs relegated each season	2

Brilliant Barça

Barcelona have won more titles than any other club. Their squad of superstars is made up of some of the best players in the women's game, from all over the world. The team is known for playing exciting, attacking football.

Liga F records

Most appearances

Barcelona – 32 seasons

Unbeaten in a season

Levante (2000–01) and Barcelona (2021–22)

Most Golden Boot trophies (all seasons)

Jenni Hermoso – 5

FOOTBALL IN GERMANY

Bundesliga

Since Germany's top men's league began in 1963, 13 different clubs have been crowned champions. The football played is fast and physical, with the whole team working hard to win back the ball quickly if they lose it. Eighteen teams battle in the Bundesliga each season.

Bundesliga records

Most appearances (all seasons)

Karl-Heinz Körbel (Eintracht Frankfurt) - 602

Most goals (all seasons)

Gerd Müller (Bayern Munich) - 365

Most goals (in one seasons)

Robert Lewandowski - 41

German giants

Bayern Munich are easily the most successful Bundesliga team. They have won more than half the championships since the league began. Between 2013 and 2023, Bayern were champions a record 11 times in a row.

Number of teams	18
Number of games each season	34
Clubs relegated each season	2-3

English striker Harry Kane joined Bayern Munich in 2023. He scored 36 goals in his first season at the club to earn the European Golden Shoe trophy.

Frauen-Bundesliga

In Germany, the top women's league is called the Frauen-Bundesliga. Fourteen teams compete from across the country, and the league boasts some of the strongest women's teams in Europe. Four different Frauen-Bundesliga clubs have won the Women's Champions League.

Number of teams	14
Number of games each season	22
Clubs relegated 2025 season	1

The Top Two

Over the last decade or so, two big clubs have ruled the competition – Bayern Munich and VfL Wolfsburg. They are always the favourites to win the league at the start each season, as they almost always finish first and second.

Frauen-Bundesliga records

Most league titles (all seasons)

FFC/Eintracht Frankfurt and VfL Wolfsburg – 7

Most goals (all seasons)

Kerstin Garefrekes – 211

Most goals (in one seasons)

Inka Grings (1999–2000) – 38

Many top players from other European countries star in the league, including English midfielder Georgia Stanway.

FOOTBALL IN ITALY

Serie A

The first season of Serie A began in Italy in 1929–30, almost one hundred years ago. The style of football played is more defensive than in other leagues and teams plan their tactics very carefully. It is considered to be one of the strongest leagues in the world. The Coppa Campioni d'Italia trophy is awarded to the winners.

Rivals AC Milan and Internazionale are two of Italy's most historic clubs.

Serie A records

Most appearances (all seasons)
Gianluigi Buffon - 657 matches

Most goals (all seasons)
Silvio Piola - 274

Most goals (in one seasons)
Gino Rossetti (Torino), Gonzalo Higuaín (Napoli) and Ciro Immobile (Lazio) – 36

Did you know?

As well as a trophy, the winning team wears the scudetto badge on their shirts the season after their victory. The badge is a small shield with the colours of the flag of Italy.

Number of teams	20
Number of games each season	38
Clubs relegated each season	3

Goalkeeper Gianluigi Buffon won Serie A a record ten times with Juventus.

Leading the way

Juventus have won more Serie A titles than any other club (36). They have been runners-up a record 21 times too. Their name 'Juventus' may mean 'youth', but their nickname is the 'Old Lady'.

Serie A Femminile

Italy's highest women's league is called Serie A for short. It was founded in 1968, although it only became fully professional for the 2022–23 season. The season is split into two parts. First, all ten teams play each other home and away, before the table is split in two. The top five teams play each other twice more, as do the bottom five teams.

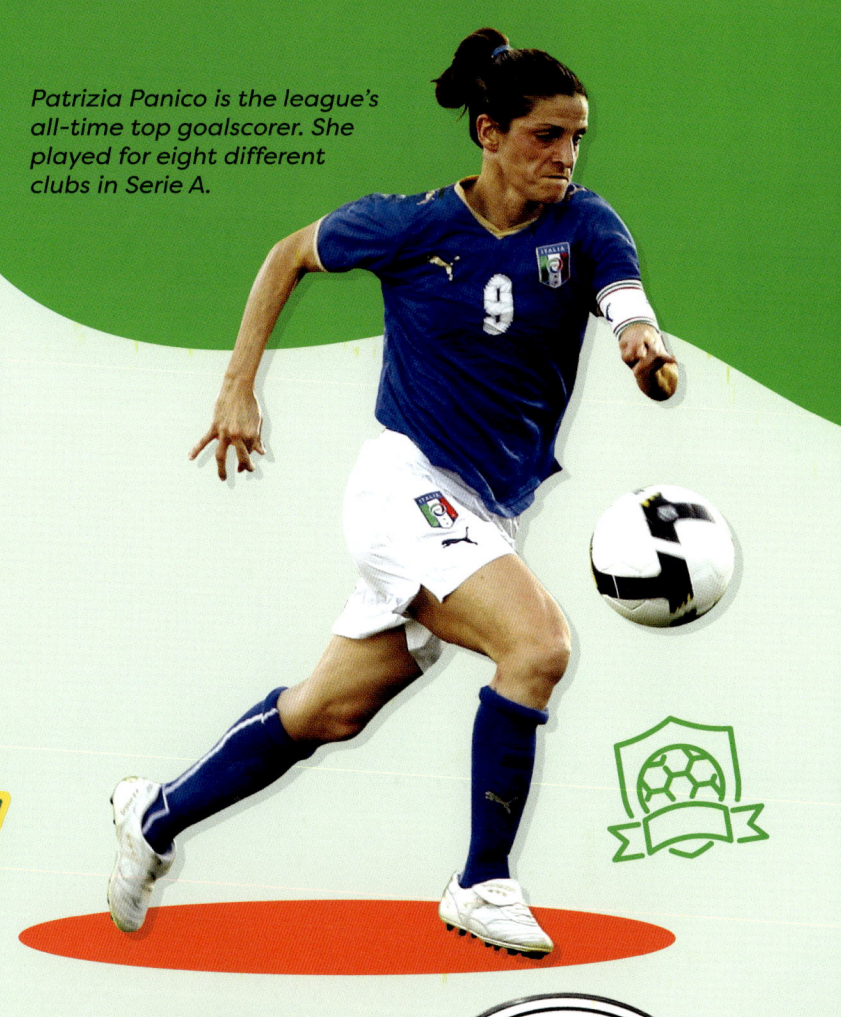

Patrizia Panico is the league's all-time top goalscorer. She played for eight different clubs in Serie A.

Number of teams	12
Number of games each season	28
Clubs relegated each season	1-2

Serie A Femminile records

Most titles (all seasons)
Torres – 7

Most goals (all seasons)
Patrizia Panico – 600+

Roma celebrate winning their second Serie A title at the end of the 2023–24 season.

FOOTBALL IN FRANCE

Ligue 1

France has had a professional league since the 1932–33 season, when 20 teams competed in a league called National and then Division 1. In 2002, the league changed its name again to Ligue 1.

Classic clubs
Only three founding member clubs still play in France's top league, almost one hundred years later – Marseille, Nice and Rennes.

Number of teams	18
Number of games each season	34
Clubs relegated each season	4

Paris Saint-Germain (in the navy kit) is the league's most successful team.

Ligue 1 records

Most appearances (all seasons)
Mickaël Landreau – 618 matches

Most goals (all seasons)
Delio Onnis – 299

Most goals (in one seasons)
Josip Skoblar (Olympique de Marseille) – 44

Did you know?
When Paris Saint-Germain bought Brazil forward Neymar Jr, from FC Barcelona, in 2017, his fee of €222 million (£200 million) made him the most expensive player in history.

Première Ligue

France's top league for women has existed for more than 50 seasons. It became known as the Première Ligue for 2024–25, when play-offs were contested between the top four clubs at the end of the season. Olympique Lyonnais (Lyon) have ruled the league over the past two decades.

Lyon won an unbeaten 14 titles in a row between 2006 and 2020.

Number of teams	12
Number of games each season	22
Clubs relegated each season	2

Première Ligue records

Most league titles

Olympique Lyonnais – 17

Most goals (in one seasons)

Sandrine Brétigny – 42

Did you know?

The Première Ligue attracts top players from abroad. USA midfielder Crystal Dunn (front row, middle) and ex-England goalkeeper Mary Earps (back row, third from left) both star for Paris Saint-Germain.

FOOTBALL IN THE UNITED STATES

Major League Soccer

Major League Soccer (MLS) is the leading league in the United States. Thirty teams make up the league, with 27 in the United States and three from Canada. They are divided between the Western and Eastern Conferences. Play began in 1996. Unlike most top leagues in football, MLS does not have promotion or relegation.

The gleaming MLS Cup.

Number of teams	30
Number of games each season	34

Two trophies

Clubs in the Eastern and Western Conferences try to win a trophy called the Supporters' Shield by earning the most points. The league's top 16 teams then compete in the play-offs for the prize of the MLS Cup.

Captain Lionel Messi and his Inter Miami team celebrate winning their first Supporters' Shield in 2024.

MLS records

Most appearances (all seasons)
Nick Rimando – 514

Most goals (all seasons)
Chris Wondolowski – 171

Most goals (in one seasons)
Carlos Vela (Los Angeles FC) – 34

National Women's Soccer League

The top women's league in the United States is known as the NWSL for short. Its first season kicked off in 2013, although two professional leagues existed before this time. Like the men's league (MLS), a play-off tournament takes place at the end of the season, after a Shield champion has been crowned.

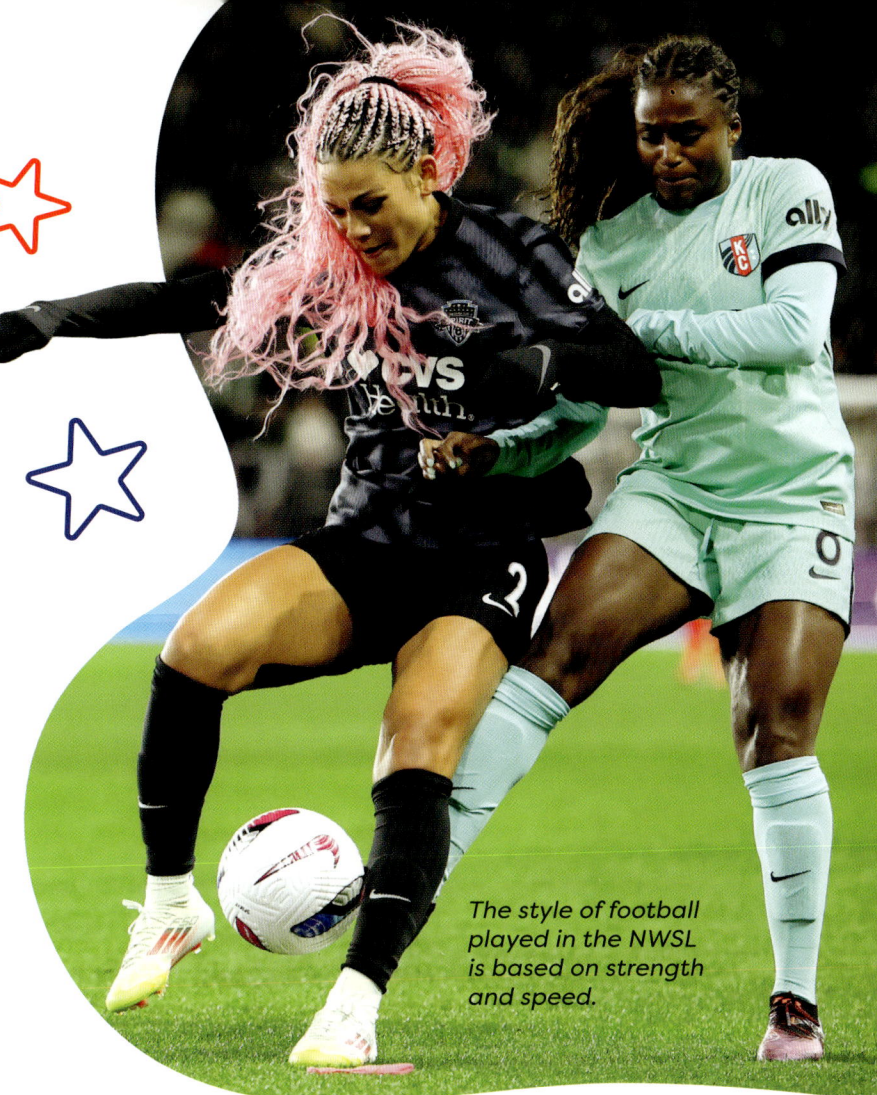

The style of football played in the NWSL is based on strength and speed.

NWSL records

Most appearances (all seasons)
Lauren Barnes – 232+ matches

Most goals (all seasons)
Lynn Biyendolo (was Williams) – 80

Most goals (in one seasons)
Temwa Chawinga (Kansas City Current) – 20

Number of teams — 14*
Number of games each season — 26**

Third trophy

The Shield winners then play the winners of the Championship (the play-off tournament) in a single cup competition called the NWSL Challenge Cup.

*16 NWSL teams will make up the league from 2026. **As of March 2025.

The Champions League

The top clubs from Europe's strongest leagues proudly compete in the Champions League. It is the most-watched club competition in the world. The tournament was first held in 1955, when it was called the European Cup and was won by Spanish club Real Madrid.

European giants Real Madrid claimed a record fifteenth Champions League title in 2024.

Champions League records

Most appearances (all seasons)
Cristiano Ronaldo – 183 matches

Most goals (all seasons)
Cristiano Ronaldo – 140

Most goals (in one seasons)
Cristiano Ronaldo – 17

Number of teams	36
Number of games each season	up to 17

Competition changes

In 2024–25, the group stage changed to a single competition with all 36 teams competing in one giant league.

*Played by the two finalists in the 2024–25 season.

The Women's Champions League

A competition for the top women's clubs in Europe was first staged in 2001–02, when it was called the 'UEFA Women's Cup'. It became the Women's Champions League in 2009–10. Every season, memorable matches are played in this **elite** competition to decide the best women's club in Europe.

History-makers

Olympique Lyonnais Féminin (Lyon Women) are the most successful club in the competition's history. They have won the trophy eight times, including a record five titles in a row from 2016 to 2020.

Number of teams	18
Number of games each season	9*

Big rivals

Barcelona have been Lyon's biggest rivals in recent years. The Spanish club won their first title in 2021 and have since added two more trophies.

Barcelona captain Alexia Putellas lifts the Women's Champions League trophy in 2024.

Women's Champions League records

Most appearances (all seasons)

Wendie Renard – 124 matches **

Most goals (all seasons)

Ada Hegerberg – 66**

Most goals (in one seasons)

Ada Hegerberg – 15

*Played by the two finalists in the 2024–25 season.
**As of March 2025.

Cup competitions

Some of the most exciting football matches take place in cup competitions, where small clubs get the chance to take on bigger and richer clubs. Games can be full of drama and comebacks, ending in shock results that are remembered for years to come.

Did you know?
Everton's Louis Saha holds the record for the fastest goal in an FA Cup final. It took him just 25 seconds to score.

The FA Cup

The FA Cup is the oldest national football competition in the world. The first final was played in 1872. Arsenal hold the record for the most victories. Their first trophy came in 1930.

The FA Cup trophy is decorated with ribbons in the colours of the winning team.

FA Cup records

Most wins (club)

Men's	Women's
Arsenal - 14	Arsenal - 14

Most wins (players)

Men's	Women's
Ashley Cole (Arsenal and Chelsea) – 7	Rachel Yankey (Arsenal and Fulham) – 11

Most wins (coach)

Men's	Women's
Arsène Wenger (Arsenal) – 7	Vic Akers (Arsenal) – 10

The Copa del Rey

The 'King's Cup' is one of the most famous cup competitions in Europe. It is the oldest competition in Spanish football. The first trophy was won in 1903. The women's version is called the Copa de la Reina or the 'Queen's Cup'.

Copa del Rey / de la Reina records

Most wins (club)

| Men's Barcelona – 32 | Women's Barcelona – 10 |

Copa Libertadores records

Most wins (club)

| Men's Independiente (Argentina) – 7 | Women's Corinthians (Brazil) – 5 |

The Copa Libertadores

The men's cup has been contested by South America's top clubs every year since 1960. Players and fans from Uruguay, Argentina, Brazil and beyond dream of winning this special trophy. 32 teams take part in the men's cup, while 16 teams play in the women's cup. The Copa Libertadores Femenina first played out in 2009.

The Club World Cup

FIFA's Club World Cup is a competition that decides the best club in the world. 32 clubs from around the globe take part. Brazilian club Corinthians won the first Club World Cup in 2000 in a penalty shoot-out.

Club World Cup records

Most wins (club)

Real Madrid – 5

Real Madrid recorded a record score of 5–3 when they beat Al-Hilal in the 2022 final.

73

More football!

As football continues to grow around the world, it inspires other versions of the game. Here are some more ways that more players and fans enjoy getting involved in the sport.

Futsal

The game of Futsal was invented in Uruguay and Brazil in South America in the 1930s. It is played indoors on a hard court. The ball used is smaller, heavier and less bouncy than a normal football. Five players make up each team. Futsal has had its own World Cup since 1989.

Futsal World Cup records

Most wins

Brazil – 6

Most appearances

Argentina, Brazil and Spain – 10

Brazil claimed their sixth World Cup victory in 2024, at the Futsal World Cup in Uzbekistan.

Did you know?

Famous footballers Lionel Messi and Neymar Jr both developed their excellent technique and ball control by playing futsal growing up.

Beach Soccer World Cup records

Most wins

Brazil – 7

Most appearances

Brazil and Japan – 12

Brazil beat Italy in the final of the Beach Soccer World Cup 2024 in the United Arab Emirates.

Beach soccer

Beach football (or soccer) is played barefoot on a small pitch made of sand. Like Futsal, teams are five-a-side with no limits on the number of substitutes. Matches last 36 minutes and are split into three thirds of 12 minutes.

Disability football

Competitions such as the Paralympic Games allow players with the same disability to compete on the big stage. Blind football is a five-a-side game for players with visual impairments. The ball makes a sound when it moves so that players can follow it.

Besides blind football, there are international competitions for those with other disabilities to enjoy the beautiful game. Versions include cerebral palsy, amputee, frame, powerchair and deaf football.

France and Argentina played out the blind football final at the Paralympic Games in 2024. France won their first gold medal.

Esports

Did you know that there is a World Cup for gamers? Some of the world's best video gamers represent their country each year at the FIFAe World Cup. Indonesia won the console trophy and Malaysia won the mobile trophy in 2024.

Team Indonesia show off their trophy at the FIFAe World Cup in 2024.

Glossary

amateur
A person or team that takes part in a sport without being paid.

assist
A pass that leads directly to a goal being scored.

attacker
Any player on the pitch whose job it is to score or assist goals.

CONCACAF
One of the six groups of countries (confederations) in world football. It represents national teams from North America, Central America and the Caribbean region.

clean sheet
When a team and its goalkeeper don't let in any goals over a whole match.

confederation
A group of countries that work together to look after football and organise tournaments in a particular region.

continental
Belonging or relating to one of the seven continents in the world.

cross
A pass made in the air or on the ground, often from wide areas into the penalty box.

defender
Players who play in the area between the goalkeeper and the midfielders.

dribble
To move the ball up the pitch, keeping it close to the body and taking lots of touches.

elite
The very best or highest-level teams, players or competitions.

formation
The way a team is set up on the pitch. The number of players in defence, midfield and attack change for different formations. The goalkeeper is not included.

forward
Players who play furthest up the pitch. They try to score or assist goals.

full-time
The end of a match. A period of extra time can be played after this if needed.

goalkeeper
The only player who can handle the ball in their own penalty area on each team. Their job is to stop goals being scored against them.

half-time
The break in between the two halves of a match. In a 90-minute match, half time lasts 15 minutes.

kick-off
The pass made from the centre spot at the start of a match or after a goal has been scored.

opposition
The other team in a game. Also called 'opponents'.

outfield
All players except for the goalkeeper.

play-off
A final contest, often between two teams over two matches, home and away.

possession
When one team has control of the ball and holds on to it by passing it around their opponents.

professional
A person or team that gets paid to play, earning enough money for it to be their job.

referee
The person in charge of a match. They make sure it follows the laws of the game.

relegation
To drop down to a lower division at the end of the season, after finishing in last place or among the bottom teams.

rivals
Two teams that compete fiercely against each other. Players and fans take the competition very seriously.

midfielder
Players who play in the middle of the pitch, between the defenders and the attackers.

pass
When a player moves the ball towards a teammate using their feet, head or chest.

red card
Shown by the referee to a player who has seriously broken the rules, meaning they have to leave the game.

shoot
To aim a kick at goal, usually while in the attacking half of the pitch.

stadium
A large structure used for outdoor sports with a pitch in the middle and seating for fans.

striker
The forward who plays furthest up the pitch. Their main job is to score goals.

substitute
A player who joins the match after it has started. They replace an injured or tired teammate or try to change the match tactics.

touchlines
The lines that mark the longest two sides of a football pitch.

tactics
The plan or actions that a coach or team chooses when playing a match.

winger
A wide midfielder who plays close to the touchline on one side of the pitch. They make crosses into the attacking penalty area.

yellow card
A warning shown by the referee to a player who has broken a law of the game.

Index

A
Africa Cup of Nations (AFCON) 54
Akers, Michelle 45
Akers, Vic 72
Ali, Almoez 55
Alves, Luís Roberto 52
Ambrois, Javier 51
Ancelotti, Carlo 10
Argentina (country) 35
Argentina (men's national team) 35, 42, 43, 50, 51, 73, 74, 75
Australia (country) 44, 45, 55

B
Ballon d'Or Féminin 31
Barcelona 34, 60, 73
Barcelona Women 61, 71, 73
Barnes, Lauren 69
Barry, Gareth 58
Bayern Munich 62, 63
Beach soccer 74
Becker, Alisson 27
Beckham, David 31
Bellingham, Jude 60
Bene, Ferenc 47
Biyendolo (was Williams), Lynn 69
Bonmatí, Aitana 31, 61
Brazil (men's national team) 42, 43, 47, 51, 66, 73, 74
Brazil (women's national team) 45, 47, 51, 53, 73
Bronze, Lucy 29
Brétigny, Sandrine 67
Buffon, Gianluigi 64
Bundesliga 62
Bundesliga 2
Burtini, Silvana 53

C
Caicedo, Linda 51
Canada (country) 43, 52, 68
Canada (women's national team) 53
Champions League 21, 70
Chawinga, Temwa 69
Chelsea Women 28, 59
Clemence, Ray 35
Coach 10, 35, 36, 49, 54, 58, 72, 77
Cole, Ashley 72
Colombia (men's national team)
Colombia (women's national team) 51
CONCACAF 53, 76
Copa América 35, 50
Copa América Femenina 51
Copa de la Reina 73
Copa del Rey 73
Copa Libertadores 73
Copa Libertadores Femenina 73
Coppa Campioni d'Italia 64
Cristiane 47, 51

D E
Daei, Ali 55
Daly, Rachel
Davies, Alphonso 29
Defenders 21, 24, 28-29, 32, 37, 77
disability football 75
Donovan, Landon 52
Dunai, Antal 47
Dunn, Crystal 67
Earps, Mary 67
Eintracht Frankfurt 62, 63
England (country) 8, 9, 10, 39, 43, 44, 48, 49, 58, 59, 67
England (men's national team) 38, 48, 58
England (women's national team) 29, 38, 49, 59, 67
esports 75
Estadio Daniel Alcides Carrión 39
Eto'o, Samuel 54

F G
FA Cup 72
Ferguson, Alex 35
FIFA 73
FIFAe World Cup 75
Finalissima 51
Fontaine, Just 43
formations 37
Formiga 45, 51
Forwards 24, 30, 32-33, 36, 37
France (men's national team) 10, 43, 48, 49, 66
France (women's national team) 67
Frauen-Bundesliga
futsal 63
Garefrekes, Kerstin 63
Germany (country) 10, 42, 43, 44, 45, 48, 49, 62, 63
Germany (men's national team) 62, 49
Germany (women's national team) 44, 45, 49, 63
Girma, Naomi 28
goal-line technology 13
goalkeepers 26-27
Gold Cup 52
Golden Boot 33, 61
Grings, Inka 49, 63
Guardiola, Pep 58

H I
Haaland, Erling 32
Hegerberg, Ada 71
Hermoso, Jenni 61
Higuaín, Gonzalo 64
Honduras (men's national team)
Immobile, Ciro 64
Iniesta, Andrés
Inter Miami 68
Internazionale 39, 64
Ireland (country) 48
Italy (country) 10, 39, 42, 48, 64, 65, 74
Italy (men's national team) 48, 64
Ivory Coast (men's national team) 54

J K
Jair 51
Japan (country) 9, 44, 45, 55, 75
Japan (men's national team) 55

Japan (women's national team) 44, 45, 55
Joaquin 60
Jung-suk, Jung 55
Juventus 64
Kane, Harry 62
Kerr, Sam 55
Klose, Miroslav 43
Körbel, Karl-Heinz 62
Kum-suk, Ri 55

L M
La Liga 60
Landreau, Mickaël 66
Lewandowski, Robert 62
Liga F 61
Ligue 1 66
Lilly, Kristine 34, 45
Major League Soccer 68
  MLS Cup 68
  MLS Supporters' Shield 68
Manchester United 58
Marta 45
Martínez, Emi 26
Maschio, Humberto 51
Matthäus, Lothar 43
Mbappé, Kylian 33
McCabe, Katie
Mead, Beth 49
Méndez, Norberto 51
Messi, Lionel 34, 42, 43, 51, 60, 68, 74
Mexico (country) 43, 52, 53
Mexico (men's national team) 52
Midfielders 24, 30-31, 37, 76
Miedema, Vivianne 47
Milan, AC 39, 64
MLS Cup 68
Mulamba, Ndaye 54
Müller, Gerd 62

N O
Naeher, Alyssa 27
Nagasato, Yūki 55
National Women's Soccer League (NWSL) 69
  NWSL Challenge Cup 69
  NWSL Championship 69
  NWSL Shield 69
New Zealand (country) 45, 53
Neymar da Silva Santos Júnior (aka Neymar Jr) 66, 74
Nielsen, Sophus 47
Nigeria (men's national team) 54
Nigeria (women's national team) 54
Nkwocha, Perpetua 54
Nobbs, Jordan 59
Norway (women's national team) 44, 45, 49
Olimpico 22
Olympic Games 46-47
Olympique Lyonnais (Lyon) 67, 71
Onnis, Delio 66

P Q
Palmer, Cole 22
Panama (men's national team) 52
Panico, Patrizia 65
Paralympic Games 75
Paris Saint-Germain (men's team) 66, 67
Pelé 7, 35
Piola, Silvio 64
Platini, Michel 49
play-off 67, 68, 69, 77
Popp, Alexandra 49
Premier League 22, 58
Première Ligue 67
Prinz, Birgit 49
Putellas, Alexia 71
Qatar (men's national team) 33, 56

R S
Real Madrid 60, 70, 73
Real Madrid Women 61
referee 12, 13, 26, 77
referee, assistant 13
Renard, Wendie 71
Rimando, Nick 68
Rodri 30
Roma Women 65
Ronaldo, Cristiano 21, 43, 49, 70
Rose Bowl stadium 38
Roseli 51
Rossetti, Gino 64
Saha, Louis 72
Salah, Mohamed 33
Sandygate stadium 39
San Siro stadium 39
Scotland (men's national team) 9, 48
Scudetto 64
Serie A 64
Serie A Femminile 65
Serie B (women's league)
Shaw, Khadija 33
Shearer, Alan 58
Sinclair, Christine 34

Skoblar, Josip 66
Song, Rigobert 54
Spain (men's national team) 10, 30, 43, 46, 48, 49, 60, 74
Spain (women's national team) 44, 45, 61, 74
Stanway, Georgia 63
Strikers 37
Substitutes 10, 74
Supporters' Shield 68
Swanson, Mallory 47

T U V
Tamires 47
Torres (women's team) 65
United States (country) 9, 43, 47, 52, 56, 68, 69
United States (women's national team) 9, 34, 44, 45, 47, 53, 56, 69
Uruguay (men's national team) 42, 43, 51, 73, 74
van Dijk, Virgil 28
Vela, Carlos 68
Vinicius Junior

W
Wales (men's national team) 48
Washington Spirit
Wembly Stadium 38
Wenger, Arsène 72
Wiegman, Sarina 49
Wolfsburg Women 63
Women's Africa Cup of Nations (WAFCON) 54
Women's Champions League 59, 63, 71
Women's Super League 59
Women's World Cup 9, 44-45, 53
Wondolowski, Chris 68
World Cup 9, 27, 33, 35, 38, 40, 42-43, 46

X Y Z
Xavi
Yankey, Rachel 72
Ying, Li 55
Yugoslavia (men's national team)
Zizinho 51
Zubizarreta, Andoni 60